Instant Apple Configurator How-to

Gain full control and complete security when managing mobile iOS devices in mass deployments

Charles Edge

TJ Houston

PUBLISHING

BIRMINGHAM - MUMBAI

Instant Apple Configurator How-to

First published: March 2013

Production Reference: 1210313

Published by Packt Publishing Ltd.
Livery Place
35 Livery Street
Birmingham B3 2PB, UK.

ISBN 978-1-84969-406-3

www.packtpub.com

Credits

Authors

Charles Edge

TJ Houston

Reviewer

Allister Banks

Acquisition Editor

Akram Hussain

Commissioning Editor

Harsha Bharwani

Technical Editor

Veronica Fernandes

Project Coordinator

Amigya Khurana

Proofreader

Maria Gould

Production Coordinator

Manu Joseph

Cover Work

Manu Joseph

Cover Image

Conidon Miranda

About the Authors

Charles Edge is the Chief Technology Officer of 318 Inc, a national, Mac-first consultancy based in Santa Monica, California. Here he manages a team of elite systems administrators who enjoy improving technology as much as they enjoy figuring out the weird things people do to computers. Charles has been involved with opening 318 offices around the United States, including a presence in New York, Nashville, Minneapolis, San Francisco, and Portland. He speaks at a number of conferences. His first speaking appearance at a large conference was DefCon 2004. Since then he has spoken at conferences such as MacSysAdmin, MacWorld, LinuxWorld, and BlackHat. He is also the author of `krypted.com`, a site dedicated to heterogeneous networking and Apple systems administration.

He has authored several books including:

- *Enterprise iPhone and iPad Administrator's Guide, Apress*, November 2010, *ISBN 1-4302-3009-6*

- *The Mac Tiger Server Little Black Book, Paraglyph Press*, February 2006, *ISBN 1-933097-14-0*

- *Web Scripting Little Black Book, Paraglyph Press*, April 2007, *ISBN 1-933097-19-1*

- *Foundations of Mac OS X Leopard Security, Apress*, March 2008, *ISBN 1-59059-989-6*

- *Foundations of Mac OS X Snow Leopard Security, Apress*, February 2010, *ISBN 1-4302-2730-3*

- *Enterprise Mac Administrator's Guide, Apress*, October 2009, *ISBN 1-4302-2443-6*

- *Beginning Mac OS X Snow Leopard Server: From Solo Install to Enterprise Integration, Apress*, February 2010, *ISBN 1-4302-2772-9*

- *Using Mac OS X Lion Server, O'Reilly*, January 2012, *ISBN 1-4493-1605-0*

TJ Houston is the Director of Technology for Huron City Schools and has worked with educators for over 5 years. A significant amount of this time has been focused on:

- Google Apps
- iOS devices (deployment and training)
- Basic computer skills
- Interactive white boards
- Video editing and multimedia

TJ has a degree in Business with a focus on IT. He is an author, blogger, podcaster, photographer, and trainer. He is passionate about helping educators and administrators learn about 21st century education as well as sharing resources that further the educational process.

I would like to thank my family, Donna, Tim, and Megan for always supporting everything I do. I also want to thank my fiancée Ashley for the support and help throughout this project.

About the Reviewer

Allister Banks is excitable, knows enough Japanese to order food, and lives with his wife in NYC. Professionally, he is a Solutions Architect for 318 in downtown NYC (and elsewhere) and maintains the InstaDMG project.

www.PacktPub.com

Support files, eBooks, discount offers and more

You might want to visit www.PacktPub.com for support files and downloads related to your book.

Did you know that Packt offers eBook versions of every book published, with PDF and ePub files available? You can upgrade to the eBook version at www.PacktPub.com and as a print book customer, you are entitled to a discount on the eBook copy. Get in touch with us at service@packtpub.com for more details.

At www.PacktPub.com, you can also read a collection of free technical articles, sign up for a range of free newsletters and receive exclusive discounts and offers on Packt books and eBooks.

http://PacktLib.PacktPub.com

Do you need instant solutions to your IT questions? PacktLib is Packt's online digital book library. Here, you can access, read and search across Packt's entire library of books.

Why Subscribe?

- ▶ Fully searchable across every book published by Packt
- ▶ Copy and paste, print and bookmark content
- ▶ On demand and accessible via web browser

Free Access for Packt account holders

If you have an account with Packt at www.PacktPub.com, you can use this to access PacktLib today and view nine entirely free books. Simply use your login credentials for immediate access.

Table of Contents

Preface

Apple Configurator is a great tool from Apple, meant to help in automating the setup and management of iOS devices for a number of environments. Although Apple Configurator is, as with most things from Apple, easy to use, it is a different way of managing devices. This book is meant to guide you through getting used to using Apple Configurator so that you can get devices in your users' hands quickly and effectively with the user experience you always knew you could give them.

What this book covers

Signing up for an Apple ID (Must know) shows how to appropriately use Apple Configurator. For this, administrators need an Apple ID. An Apple ID is the same kind of account used to purchase music through iTunes, use iCloud to send images to photo stream, and log in to the Apple developer portal. The Apple ID is critical if any applications are to be imported into Apple Configurator as well as in order to download the tool from the Mac App Store in the first place.

Installing Apple Configurator (Must know) explains how to download and install Apple Configurator. Apple Configurator is a free tool that can only be downloaded via the Mac App Store. Once downloaded, it can be distributed to as many machines as needed.

Configuring the Apple Configurator preferences (Should know) walks you through the preference panes for Apple Configurator, including the ability to set lock screen images, show usernames on locked devices, and set notification sounds.

Migrating existing profiles into Apple Configurator (Should know) explains that iPhone Configuration Utility was the first tool available for managing iOS devices. Many environments have already built complicated workflows leveraging profiles from iPhone Configuration Utility. In this recipe, we look at migrating those profiles from iPhone Configuration Utility and into Apple Configurator, so you don't have to redo all the hard work put into the old way of doing things.

Deciding whether to prepare, supervise, or assign (Must know) shows us a number of ways to use Apple Configurator. If we compare the Prepare and Supervise modes, we see that it's all about the paid apps. If you don't need to distribute apps, supervise. The Assign mode is used when it's all about the documents in the apps, if you don't need to distribute content.

Creating a cart workflow (Should know) covers some of the topics that should be looked at once Apple Configurator has been installed and you've had a chance to play with it.

Leveraging Configurator in a one-to-one environment (Should know) shows how many schools are moving to a model where every child has a device. This is similar to how companies have done IT for decades. If these are iOS devices, Apple Configurator will play some role in their setup.

Checking out devices (Should know) explains the workflow in which iOS devices are checked out from a central point to many different users.

Creating a device backup (Should know) tells us that the most basic feature for anyone working on a large deployment (which can be anywhere from 10 to 100,000 devices) needs to master is how to take a device in a given state and replicate that state exactly as the device was onto another device. This is usually referred to as imaging. In an iOS world, we call it backup and restore and can use iTunes or Apple Configurator for the task. The first step is to create a device backup.

Restoring a device backup (Should know) explains that once administrators have a good backup of a device, it's time to restore that backup onto another device. In fact, the backup can be restored to up to 30 devices concurrently.

Understanding profiles (Become an expert) shows that the best way to understand what a profile is, is to open up one and look at it. In this recipe we'll take a profile and view the layout and structure.

Building a profile (Must know) explains that the most common element most administrators want to give devices is access to a wireless network. This could be a complicated 802.1x environment where a certificate and other elements are placed into the profile, or it could be as simple as a WPA2 environment hosted on an Apple AirPort. In this recipe, we'll take a look at the basic WPA profile as initially seeding devices (for example, for later enrollment into Mobile Device management solutions).

Exploring all profiles (Should know) explains that the profiles available in Apple Configurator control how passcodes are enforced, push certificates to devices, place web clips (or links that look like apps) on home screens, and can limit various things the device can do, such as disabling the camera or even the home button. In this recipe, we will step through the various options available to administrators as well as when you might not want to use some (such as disabling the App Store before you install apps).

Exporting profiles (Must know) shows us how to export management profiles from Configurator to be used with other deployment tools.

Creating auto enrollment profiles (Become an expert) shows that Apple Configurator can automatically enroll devices into Mobile Device Management (MDM) solutions, such as JAMF's Casper or Apple's Profile Manager.

Purchasing applications through the VPP (Should know) explains how you can use the Volume Purchasing Program (VPP). VPP is available to Apple customers in the United States and allows schools and companies to purchase application codes that can then be redeemed to tie an application to an Apple ID. In some cases, VPP will give discounts to purchasers for applications purchased in bulk, but not all.

Importing applications (Should know) shows how each app that will be deployed through Apple Configurator must initially be imported into the tool. Doing so makes a copy of the app in Apple Configurator.

Deploying applications on prepared devices (Become an expert) explains how apps from the App Store can be deployed when restoring devices through Apple Configurator.

Deploying applications on managed devices (Become an expert) shows how deploying apps on managed devices is the only way to hand out Volume Purchasing Program (VPP) codes in a way that the codes can be taken back. When apps are pushed to managed devices, the VPP code is not associated with the end user's Apple ID. This means that when the device is checked back in, the VPP code will be ready for use on a different device.

Adding files to devices (Should know) shows us how to add files to different applications easily through Apple Configurator.

Importing files back to the computer (Should know), shows how we can receive documents from a user or a device. Whether device supervision is being leveraged in a computer lab in a company or for a cart on wheels in a school district, once the devices have been used for a time, they will invariably end up with data on them.

What you need for this book

In this book, we cover the installation and management of Apple Configurator, but Apple Configurator is a tool used for mass deployment, and when managing large numbers of devices, no amount of planning is enough. Before using this book, as a means of preparing and managing devices, consider the user experience and the painstaking detail that goes into the stock configuration of an iOS device.

Apple makes a lot of choices on behalf of users. You will be altering this user experience. Make sure that you understand what goes into each aspect of doing so. For example, if you are preparing devices and lock them down too far, what's to keep your users from wiping devices and attempting to recreate your planned experience for them in a less restrictive environment?

This book explores the limitations and capabilities when using Apple Configurator, but please keep in mind that the more you plan the user experience, the more that care and feeding shows in how that experience is received. The popularity of iOS-based devices is immense. This is for a reason and we caution you not to lock devices down too much, but to be very premeditated in the experience you provide to your users. In short, measure twice and cut once.

In addition to good planning, you'll also need at least one iOS device and at least one OS X computer. The computer will run Apple Configurator and the iOS device will perform all the necessary automations to test a complete iOS deployment.

Who this book is for

Apple Configurator is a tool meant to aid in the use and management en masse of Apple devices. This book is intended for administrators and users of large-scale iOS implementations. This includes receptionists, school teachers, network administrators, business owners, and others charged with preparing, supervising, and assigning devices to users, whether this means 10 or 10,000 devices.

Conventions

In this book, you will find a number of styles of text that distinguish between different kinds of information. Here are some examples of these styles, and an explanation of their meaning.

Code words in text are shown as follows: "Profiles should not be encrypted and should be saved in the .mobileconfig format to be imported."

New terms and **important words** are shown in bold. Words that you see on the screen, in menus or dialog boxes for example, appear in the text like this: "Then provide a billing address and click on the **Create Apple ID** button at the bottom of the screen."

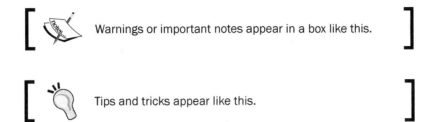

Warnings or important notes appear in a box like this.

Tips and tricks appear like this.

Reader feedback

Feedback from our readers is always welcome. Let us know what you think about this book—what you liked or may have disliked. Reader feedback is important for us to develop titles that you really get the most out of.

To send us general feedback, simply send an e-mail to feedback@packtpub.com, and mention the book title via the subject of your message.

If there is a book that you need and would like to see us publish, please send us a note in the **SUGGEST A TITLE** form on www.packtpub.com or e-mail suggest@packtpub.com.

If there is a topic that you have expertise in and you are interested in either writing or contributing to a book, see our author guide on www.packtpub.com/authors.

Customer support

Now that you are the proud owner of a Packt book, we have a number of things to help you to get the most from your purchase.

Errata

Although we have taken every care to ensure the accuracy of our content, mistakes do happen. If you find a mistake in one of our books—maybe a mistake in the text or the code—we would be grateful if you would report this to us. By doing so, you can save other readers from frustration and help us improve subsequent versions of this book. If you find any errata, please report them by visiting http://www.packtpub.com/support, selecting your book, clicking on the **errata submission form** link, and entering the details of your errata. Once your errata are verified, your submission will be accepted and the errata will be uploaded on our website, or added to any list of existing errata, under the Errata section of that title. Any existing errata can be viewed by selecting your title from http://www.packtpub.com/support.

Piracy

Piracy of copyright material on the Internet is an ongoing problem across all media. At Packt, we take the protection of our copyright and licenses very seriously. If you come across any illegal copies of our works, in any form, on the Internet, please provide us with the location address or website name immediately so that we can pursue a remedy.

Please contact us at `copyright@packtpub.com` with a link to the suspected pirated material.

We appreciate your help in protecting our authors, and our ability to bring you valuable content.

Questions

You can contact us at `questions@packtpub.com` if you are having a problem with any aspect of the book, and we will do our best to address it.

Instant Apple Configurator How-to

Welcome to *Instant Apple Configurator How-to*. This book is a guide on managing iOS devices en masse using the tools Apple provides for us to do so. Apple Configurator can fill a few different roles within your environment. One is as an imaging tool, another is as a tool that locks down devices (similar to how iPhone Configuration Utility was used, previously), and finally there is the ability to distribute content (whereby content is apps and documents within apps, in our opinion).

Signing up for an Apple ID (Must know)

Apple Configurator can be used without an Apple ID. However, an Apple ID is required to manage apps on a device and for purchasing Apple Configurator on the Mac App Store prior to using the tool. In this section, we will sign up for an Apple ID.

Getting ready

Before signing up for an Apple ID, you will need a functional e-mail address. Optionally, a valid credit card number enables you to purchase apps from the iOS App Store, if needed. Once all required apps have been purchased, you can remove the credit card information from the Apple ID if you wish.

The easiest way to create an Apple ID is to purchase an app. This turns out to be the only way to create an Apple ID without a credit card number, a must in many environments. To create an Apple ID with a credit card number is a similar process, but not required.

 It is worth noting that if you require an Apple ID without a credit card you must purchase a free app (`http://support.apple.com/kb/HT2534`).

How to do it...

For this demo we will be purchasing a free app (iBooks), so we can create an Apple ID without a credit card.

1. Open iTunes.
2. Click on the iTunes Store link in the iTunes sidebar.
3. On the iTunes Store screen, search for iBooks.
4. When prompted to sign in, click on the **Create Apple ID** button, shown in the following screenshot:

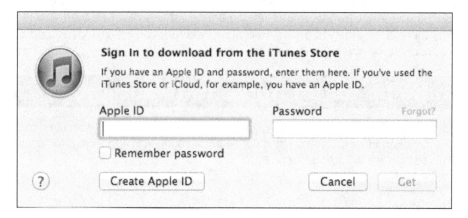

5. At the **Welcome to the iTunes Store** screen, click on the **Continue** button. You will then be prompted to accept the Apple Licensing Agreement. Here, check the **I have read and agree to these terms and conditions** checkbox (assuming of course that you agree to the terms) and then click on the **Agree** button.

6. At the **Provide Apple ID Details** screen, enter the appropriate information, which includes the following:

   ❑ **Email**: A valid e-mail address that is unique for the Apple ID.
   ❑ **Password**: The password used to authenticate the new account.

- ❑ **Verify Password**: The password provided a second time so as to keep us from having typos in the **Password** field.

- ❑ **Security Info**: Three questions and answers to be used for account recovery purposes.

- ❑ **Optional Rescue Email**: A second e-mail address used to reset the account in case it is locked out.

- ❑ **Date of Birth**: A date that should be at least 13 years before the date the account is being created (for example, the date a school was founded or the actual date a person was born).

7. Once the appropriate fields are filled out, click on the **Continue** button. At the **Provide a Payment Method** screen, click on **None**. Then provide a billing address and click on the **Create Apple ID** button at the bottom of the screen.

A verification e-mail is then sent to the e-mail address used. Click on the **Verify Now** link in that e-mail to complete the setup of the Apple ID. On the Apple ID site, simply enter the username and password for the newly created Apple ID to complete the setup.

How it works...

You now have a functional Apple ID. This ID can be used to access a variety of services from Apple. The most important of these services for this book is to access the Mac App Store and the iOS App Store and associate apps with VPP codes, which we'll cover later in this book.

There's more...

An Apple ID can be used for way more than just purchasing VPP codes and downloading free apps. Apple IDs are the gateway to most Apple services, providing access to iCloud, logging into the Apple forums, information about certifications, gaining access to the developer portal, and more. For more information on Apple IDs, check out `http://www.apple.com/support/appleid`.

Bulk account creation

As many environments need to create Apple IDs in bulk, it is important to note that creating more than five from a given IP address in a short period of time will set off alarms within Apple's fraud alert system. Therefore, before creating Apple IDs in bulk, make sure to update your Apple Systems Engineer that you will be doing so. This will allow Apple to whitelist you so you do not run into issues creating multiple IDs.

You can also find scripted solutions at Enterprise iOS (`http://enterpriseios.com/wiki/Batch_Apple_ID_Creator`).

Removing credit card information from an Apple ID

When using a shared account, one of the last things you want is for users to actually buy media with that shared account. It's simple to remove a credit card from the account by following these simple steps:

1. Open iTunes.
2. Click on the Apple ID in the upper right-hand corner of the screen (the e-mail address the account was registered with, usually) and select **Account** from the drop-down list, as seen in the following screenshot:

3. Once the account page loads, click on **Edit** beside the payment type.
4. On the **Edit Payment Information** screen, click on **None**.
5. Then click on **Done**.

Now there will not be a payment funding source attached to the account any longer. This can cause a few minor issues with deployments, but turns out way better than having tons of unauthorized purchases under the account.

Finding the Apple ID for purchased apps

It is usually best to start using Apple Configurator on a new user account. By utilizing a new account, you start with a fresh iTunes library. However if you are utilizing a user account that is already in use, you can easily find which Apple ID was used to purchase/download the app. If there are apps in iTunes, click on them and choose **Get Info** from the iTunes File menu to see the modification date, purchase date, purchased by, and account name (Apple ID) of each app. Keep in mind that when apps are installed by Apple Configurator, the Apple ID shown in the **Get Info** menu for the app is the Apple ID used whenever users go to update the app from the App Store when updates are available. Without that password, users will be unable to update apps on their devices.

Installing Apple Configurator (Must know)

Once you have an Apple ID, you can install Apple Configurator. The tool is a free download from the Mac App Store and can be used on as many computers as needed. Once installed, computers can be cloned if additional Apple Configurator stations are needed.

Getting ready

Apple Configurator is a free application distributed through the Mac App Store. Every Apple ID has a valid Mac App Store account. The application is a self-contained application bundle. Once purchased, copying the application bundle from one computer to another copies the installation of Apple Configurator. However, updating the application then requires the credentials for the Apple ID used to perform the initial purchase. You will also need an Apple computer as Apple Configurator only runs on Mac OS X 10.7.5 and higher at this time.

How to do it...

To install Apple Configurator, follow the given steps:

1. Open the Mac App Store.
2. Once opened, click in the search field in the upper right-hand corner of the screen and search for `apple configurator`.

 In the search results, Apple Configurator should be the only tool available.

3. Click on the **Install** button for Apple Configurator to start the download of the software.
4. In order to download, you will be prompted for an Apple ID and password. Here, enter the information for the account previously created. Then click on the **Install** button to authorize the download.

Once installed, Apple Configurator is available in the `Applications` directory as well as through Launchpad. Open Apple Configurator and accept the licensing agreement to see the splash screen, which shows the initial options available to administrators.

How it works...

Once downloaded and installed, Apple Configurator should be customized to perform a variety of tasks, which we will outline in subsequent sections of this book. The software can be downloaded using the same Apple ID to multiple computers or copied between computers.

There's more...

A key aspect of the Apple experience for both iOS and OS X moving forward is the App Store. The App Store is the gateway to applications vetted by Apple. These include tools to manage personal finances, keep track of your health, build sleek graphics, network with your friends online, keep up with the news, educate yourself about nearly anything, and of course be productive at work. Search for pretty much anything you can think of and there's a good chance that you'll find "an app for that".

Before you click, prepare...

A common mistake made when first using Apple Configurator is to configure some settings and then click on **Prepare**, the button that runs along the bottom of the screen. When that button is clicked, Apple Configurator starts watching the USB port of the Apple computer running Apple Configurator aggressively. Any iOS devices that get plugged into the computer will, if the workflow has any erase or restore options enabled, wipe the device immediately once docked. Therefore, it is critical that there is no data on the devices used to test and configure. Many people make the mistake of docking a device to Apple Configurator, if only for a second (for example, for a quick charge), only to have their personal phones or iPads wiped.

Configuring the Apple Configurator preferences (Should know)

Once installed, there is some fine-tuning left to do in Apple Configurator. Various preferences allow for tweaking how devices are supervised, the lock screens of devices, and sounds that the system can play.

Getting ready

Before configuring the preferences, Apple Configurator must be installed. The OS X computer should also be bound to the directory service being used.

How to do it...

To set up the Apple Configurator preferences, open Launchpad or open Apple Configurator from the `/Applications` directory and then click on **Preferences** from the Apple Configurator menu.

1. At the General screen, configure the following options:

   □ **When a supervised device is connected**: The **Automatically refresh** option refreshes supervised devices when they are docked, provided the system is in **Refresh** mode. **Refresh** mode is only available under the **Supervise** option.

   □ **When a supervised device is refreshed**: The **Remove apps and profiles Configurator did not install** option gives administrators the option to either leave data that wasn't put on devices through Configurator in place when supervising devices, or remove the apps (and the data in the apps) when configuring the iOS device for supervision.

- ❏ **Play sound on completion**: Configures a sound to play each time a device is finished being prepared or supervised.
- ❏ **Reset all dialog warnings**: The **Reset Warnings** button re-enables each of the warning dialogs that have been suppressed in Apple Configurator.

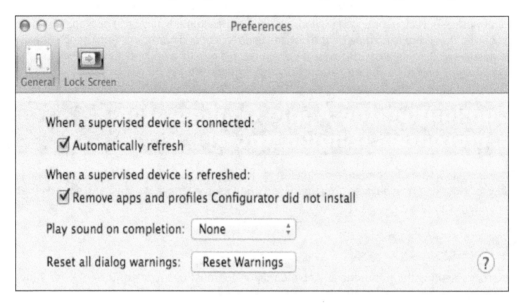

2. Next, click on **Lock Screen** from the toolbar of the preference window on the **Preferences** screen. Here, you can configure how the lock screen behaves for iPhone and iPad when the devices are supervised. The **Text** field allows for configuring what information is displayed on supervised devices. The options in the **Text** field include:

- ❏ **None**: Leaves the lock screen untouched by supervision (the background has all of the attributes the restore had)
- ❏ **Device or user name**: Leverages data from the directory service for the name of users associated to devices during supervision
- ❏ **Custom**: Sets a text string as the background (for example, `Property of Lumpkin County High School`)

Additionally, use the **Include user image** checkbox shown in the following screenshot to pull a picture of users from the directory service during supervision and place that on the lock screen as well:

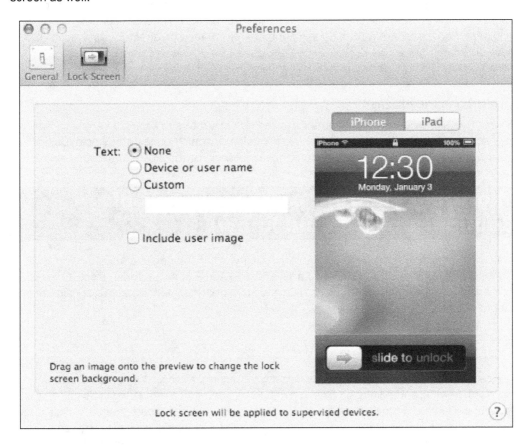

How it works...

Once all of your preferences are configured as you wish, close the **Preferences** screen to commit your changes.

There's more...

A directory service is a database of users, groups, passwords, and the resources those objects access, such as printers, file shares, and even home directory locations. User names in Apple Configurator are pulled from OS X Server. For more information on directory services in OS X, check out `http://manuals.info.apple.com/en_US/OpenDirAdmin_v10.6.pdf`. The document is a little old but mostly still applicable.

Apple ID association

The initial versions of Apple Configurator allowed administrators to assign an Apple ID that was used to link to the App Store. In the latest version of Apple Configurator, Apple IDs are only taken from each app and no key exchange is required by the global application.

Migrating existing profiles into Apple Configurator (Should know)

Profiles can be created in iPhone Configuration Utility, Profile Manager, and third-party MDM solutions, programmatically (through scripts) and with Apple Configurator. In some cases, a lot of time and effort went into creating profiles and so recreating them will take a considerable amount of time.

Getting ready

Before importing a profile, you'll first need to have a profile to import. While we haven't discussed creating and editing profiles in this book yet (we will), we're going to assume that you've exported a profile from one of the many apps that can create them and that you have permission to access the file. This is very helpful though, if you've configured a number of different profiles in iPhone Configuration Utility and are transitioning into Apple Configurator, a common task. Profiles should not be encrypted and should be saved in the .mobileconfig format to be imported.

How to do it...

1. To import a profile, click on **Prepare** in Apple Configurator. Then, click on the plus sign and then on **Import Profile...** as seen in the following screenshot:

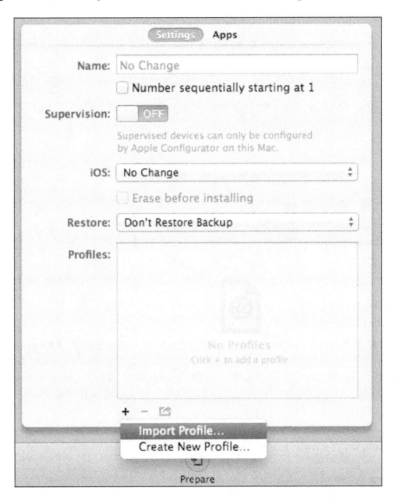

2. At the **Select Configuration Profiles** screen, browse to the profile you will be importing as shown in the following screenshot:

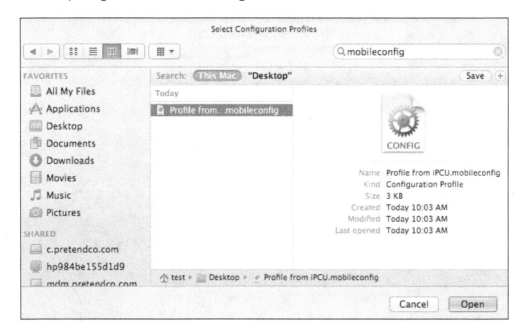

How it works...

Profiles are XML files, saved in the `.mobileconfig` format. For those with experience with OS X, these are similar to the standard Apple Property List (`.plist`) files used to configure settings within OS X. As mentioned previously, profiles should not be encrypted or Apple Configurator cannot read them. However, Apple Configurator can import profiles that have been "signed".

There's more...

XML, or Extensible Markup Language, has become the defacto standard for managing many forms of information both for the Web, iOS, and OS X. The `.mobileconfig` files in OS X are similar, as mentioned, to `.plist` files. The `.mobileconfig` files can also be created in the iPhone Configuration Utility. Both `.plist` and `.mobileconfig` files can be edited using tools like defaults. For more information on doing so, check out `http://krypted.com/ iphone/exporting-information-from-iphone-configuration-utility`.

Enrolling in Mobile Device Management

Profiles can also be used to automate enrollment into Apple's Profile Manager (built into OS X Server) and third-party MDM solutions. When enrolling in these services, profiles need to be installed on devices, which then are configured to trust and routinely check in with the MDM solution. The MDM solution needs to be accessible to the devices when the profiles are installed, meaning that these profiles frequently need to also have a Wi-Fi password as a payload as well.

Deciding whether to prepare, supervise, or assign (Must know)

Apple Configurator has three modes. They are as follows:

- ▶ **Prepare**: This is used to push settings, profiles, and applications to devices once, but the device will not be bringing data back to the Configurator system. Prepare can also be used to update to new versions of iOS, wipe devices, and even load custom builds of iOS (for example, betas) onto devices.

- ▶ **Supervise**: This can do everything that Prepare can do, but can also be used to pull volume licensed application codes back to the device.

- ▶ **Assign**: This requires a directory service, and can do everything available in Prepare and Supervise, but can also be used to distribute documents and other data to devices.

If you are supervising or assigning devices, you cannot then sync those devices in iTunes. This means that all content that is destined for the device should be distributed via Apple Configurator.

Getting ready

Before setting up anything in Apple Configurator, plan the exact user experience that you want users to have. This can be how you want students, teachers, trainees in companies, or employees to interact with these devices. Once you know exactly how you want the devices to be used, it is much easier to configure them en masse. Any slight change to how they are to be used is problematic to scale.

How to do it...

Apple Configurator can move between various modes by simply clicking on each mode at the top of the screen. Click on each to see the options available under each.

How it works...

Apple Configurator is a great tool for performing the initial setup on devices. However, it does not plan how you are going to use these devices in the first place. In order to get to the point where Apple Configurator can do what you need, first make sure to know what you need your devices to do. Go through each option in Configurator (there really aren't that many) and get comfortable with the tool and understand how it really works, at least at the GUI level.

There's more...

This book explores planning a deployment in much more depth and we then move into leveraging backups. We will also explore using profiles in much more depth, and look at application installation as well.

Now that you have set up Configurator, take some time and think through how you will be using your devices with Configurator. With your end result in mind, you have to decide whether your devices will be a classroom set, handed out to individuals for long-term use, or checked out in a library situation. No matter your end goal, there is a workflow for your environment. As we go ahead we will go more in depth with concepts introduced in the following recipe.

Creating a cart workflow (Should know)

The cart workflow is designed around the devices used throughout the day and brought back to a single sync point such as a cart or tray.

Getting ready

Before creating a workflow designed around a cart, determine how your users are going to utilize the iOS devices. It is recommended you set up one device and configure your settings until you get the device exactly how you want it and then push it out via Configurator.

How to do it...

To create a classroom set, you must first set up your naming scheme. To do so:

1. Open Apple Configurator.
2. Click on **Prepare**.
3. Now in the name area, enter the name of your devices.

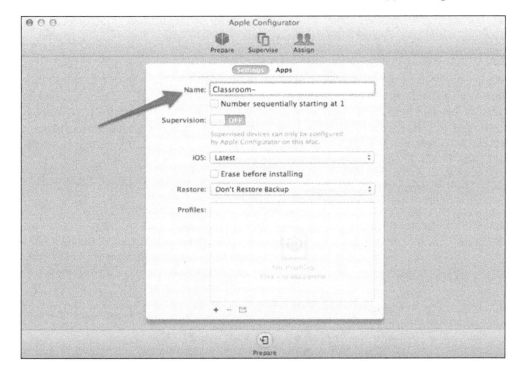

 By checking the box below the **Name** field you can incrementally number devices by adding a number after the name.

In the preface we discussed whether to supervise the devices or not; choose what will work for you. Remember devices that are under supervision can only be managed by the Mac they are supervised by. This includes iTunes content.

4. Next, select if you would like the iOS version to be updated to the newest available release. This is a great way to update many devices at once.

 The box below iOS will erase the device before updating the iOS version. This box will be grayed out unless iOS is set to the latest version.

Post this we see the backup section where we go more in depth into backing up and restoring from backups.

The last section is the profile section. Profiles are used for setting up specific settings as well as restrictions. Later on we explore the depths with profiles including adding third-party profiles such as Casper, and Meraki.

Users are always finding new applications to be added to the devices. Much like classrooms, companies will need certain applications put on all devices; this can be a daunting task but luckily Configurator helps with this task. We go more in depth in the *Deploying applications on prepared devices (Become an expert)* and *Deploying applications on managed devices (Become an expert)* recipes. Click on **Prepare**.

Configurator monitors the computer's USB port. Any time a device is plugged in, Configurator will take over and set up the devices. It's important to note that if you are charging your personal devices, they will also be subjected to Configurator and possibly delete all of your content.

How it works...

The cart workflow allows administrators/teachers the ability to control devices en masse and make changes as needed. In this workflow, all of the devices come back to one sync point.

 If you supervise a device, you can only make changes to that device with the computer it was supervised with. This can be a hassle if you are deploying the devices to sales teams across the country or classrooms across town.

Supervised devices can only be configured by Apple Configurator on this Mac.

Leveraging Configurator in a one-to-one environment (Should know)

In the previous recipe we talked about naming devices, setting up profiles, and so on. In this recipe, we will utilize what we discussed in the last section and build upon that.

Getting ready

A one-to-one environment is where each user is assigned a device and they do not come back to a centralized point to make configuration changes. Classrooms and companies are similar when it comes to managing devices in a one-to-one kind of environment. Users typically take devices home with them, personalize their own devices, and have different needs. This is important when it comes to designing your workflow; you don't want to supervise a device that people are going to take home with them, as they will not be able to change the content.

Before getting started with setting up your one-to-one workflow, make sure you have any VPP codes that you may need for paid applications that you will be installing on the devices.

How to do it...

With the one-to-one approach, many companies/schools have certain applications they want installed, but they realize the power of iOS devices is the multitude of applications that are available to end users. Many schools deploy a standard set of applications in a layered approach in which they install the apps (layer 1) and then from deployment on students can add their own iTunes account information and install their own apps.

After you are a member of VPP, you can log in to your VPP account and download a spreadsheet (.csv) of redemption codes that you can add to Configurator. We go more in depth later for installing and managing applications.

	A	B	C	D	E	F	G	I	J	K	L	M
1	Volume Purchase Codes											
2	Order ID		MU83HAU3HGV									
3	Product		Numbers, v1.6.2									
4	Purchaser		TJ Houston TJ Houston <thouston@huron-city.k12.oh.us>									
5	Codes Purchased		5									
6	Codes Redeemed		0									
7	Codes Remaining		5									
8												
9												
10	Code		Code Redemption Link									
11	AW8QRPP4WP97		https://buy.itunes.apple.com/WebObjects/MZFinance.woa/wa/freeProductCodeWizard?code=AW8QRPP4WP97									
12	M5TRENW6R34F		https://buy.itunes.apple.com/WebObjects/MZFinance.woa/wa/freeProductCodeWizard?code=M5TRENW6R34F									
13	WPXUILTAFX9N		https://buy.itunes.apple.com/WebObjects/MZFinance.woa/wa/freeProductCodeWizard?code=WPXUILTAFX9N									
14	E36O56VK9AL3		https://buy.itunes.apple.com/WebObjects/MZFinance.woa/wa/freeProductCodeWizard?code=E36O56VK9AL3									
15	PWQQLMXMME6J		https://buy.itunes.apple.com/WebObjects/MZFinance.woa/wa/freeProductCodeWizard?code=PWQQLMXMME6J									
16												

In a few recipes later in this book we will go into depth installing applications via Configurator.

 Most applications are rather inexpensive in the App Store. Think of them like office supplies. Often people make a big deal about getting applications back that they paid for. Most businesses supply employees with pens yet at the end of the quarter they do not try to get the ink back. Applications are consumable.

How it works...

The one-to-one workflow allows managers/administrators the ability to control and configure devices while allowing users the freedom of customizing and making the device their own.

There's more...

In order to install paid applications in Configurator, you must be enrolled in VPP. You can find more information about VPP on Apple's website:

▶ **Education**: http://www.apple.com/education/volume-purchase-program/

▶ **Business**: http://www.apple.com/business/vpp/

One-to-one for elementary schools

One of the unique aspects of elementary schools is that users are too young to have Apple IDs. Therefore, when doing a one-to-one for children of age 12 and under, applications must be installed on the devices by parents or administrators. Children of age 12 and under do not have the freedom of having their own account and downloading their own content.

Checking out devices (Should know)

Checking out devices allows multiple people to use iOS devices while keeping a record of the user's application data and settings so that they can be restored. When you check out the device to someone, Configurator sets up the device to the user's saved configuration and restores application data as well as other user defined settings, if present. The check-in workflow is similar to roaming profiles in enterprise environments.

Getting ready

It has been repeated over and over but that is because it is important; a supervised device can only be configured by Apple Configurator on the Mac it was originally set up with.

Supervised devices can only be configured
by Apple Configurator on this Mac.

How to do it...

The first thing you need to do to check out a device is get the device under supervision.

1. Connect your device and enter the needed information into the prepare screen.
2. Check the box for supervision.

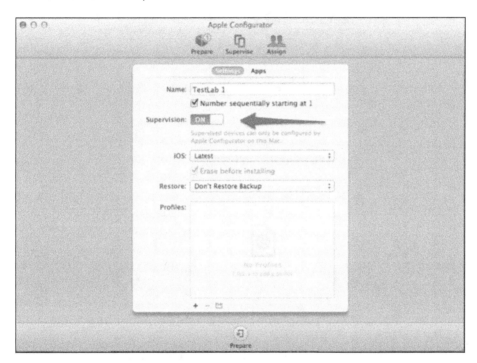

 All data on the device will be deleted.

3. When the device is under supervision, you will see a number appear next to the supervise icon.

4. Click on the supervision tab. You can now make more configuration changes on this screen, including applications. We get in depth with the application installation later. If you want to put Word documents, text documents, PDF files, or other objects not natively supported by iOS, you must first install an application that will open the file type. We will talk more about file additions in the later recipes.

5. Click on **Apply**.

6. After a device has been supervised, click on the **Assign** button.

7. On the **Assign** screen, you will see three columns:

   ❑ **Groups**

   ❑ **Users**

   ❑ **Documents**

In this area you can populate your users by clicking on the plus button at the bottom of the file. Your users can be specific or general. You may have an accounting department that has certain needs or a grade level classroom that you want to preload with content. In that case you may want to create generic users.

To learn more about adding documents and adding files, check out the recipes that follow.

8. After you are ready to check out the device to a user, click on the user and then click on the **Check Out** button.

9. When you click on the **Check Out** button, a new screen will appear. On this screen, you can choose which device will be assigned to the user.

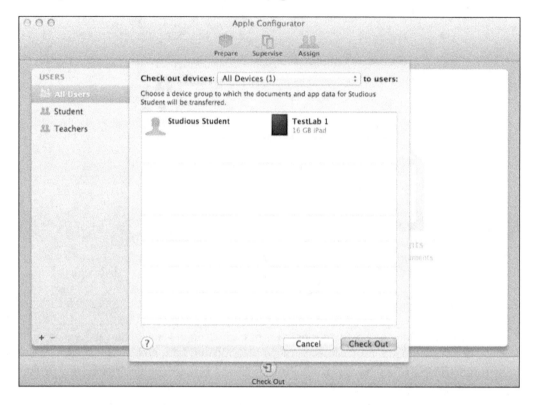

10. Click on **Check Out**.

11. To check in a device, simply plug the device back into the Mac that was originally used to configure the device. Click back to the assign pane. At the bottom, simply click on the **Check In** button.

By default, when you connect an iOS device that is supervised to Apple Configurator, any applications that were installed by the user will be deleted. This setting can be changed in the preferences menu by selecting **Preferences...** in the **Apple Configurator** menu.

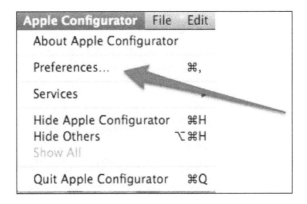

12. By unchecking the last box you ensure applications as well as profiles stay on the device.

How it works...

When devices are checked back in, Configurator backs up data contained in the applications the user has interacted with.

When we think of traditional imaging, we think of reformatting hard drives, laying files on those drives, and then automating binding to a directory service and renaming computers. Imaging an iOS device is a much simpler affair. For the most part, the operating system of an iOS device never gets touched. This means there are gigabytes of data that do not need to be put on devices and that the image which we refer to as a backup on an iOS device is just what you've done to the device since opening the box or performing a factory restore.

In this section, we're going to look at creating a backup of a device and using Apple Configurator to restore that backup in a zero touch deployment model. This means plugging the device into a computer running Apple Configurator and getting a device "imaged" without touching any buttons on the computer or clicking on the device; perfect for installing a dozen or a few thousand devices in the least amount of time possible!

Creating a device backup (Should know)

This recipe covers building out a device backup. The backup is a file used to then restore devices, covered in subsequent recipes. Once Apple Configurator is installed, this is the first step in any deployment workflow and includes any tasks concerned with personalizing devices, such as setting the device background, and icon positioning.

Getting ready

The device backup is what is restored to devices. It is best to activate a device and, without changing any options, make a backup. Then, before building the backup you will likely use for mass deployment, configure a clean device, which can be referred to as the **golden master** with all of the settings that you want the device to have. The most common things that get put into a device backup are a custom background, device icons (or badges) placed into specific folders, and any global settings.

The device backup does not contain apps, settings for apps, and should not contain items that can be placed into a profile, such as wireless networks the device will join, and certificates. The backup does retain icon placement on the screen depending on what applications are being installed.

How to do it...

1. Once an iOS device has been configured in such a way that you want others to be, dock the device into the computer with Apple Configurator installed. To create a backup, open Apple Configurator.

2. Click on the **Prepare** button along the top row of icons to see the **Prepare** screen, as shown in the following screenshot:

3. From the **Prepare** screen, click on the field for **Restore**.

4. Select **Back Up...** from the menu to access the **Which device would you like to back up?** screen as shown in the following screenshot.

5. Here, choose the device that you would like to back up (if there is only one device plugged in, then there will only be one option).

6. Click on the **Create Backup...** button.

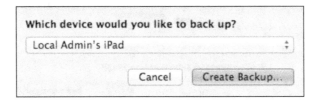

7. At the next screen, select where you want the backup to be stored and provide a name for the backup.
8. Click on **Save**. The backup should be created quickly.

Once finished, the backup is displayed in the **Restore** field and you can either repeat the process to get various iterations of backups created or move on to restoring backups in the next section.

How it works...

Once exported, profiles are stored as `.mobileconfig` files, which are similar to property lists in OS X. Device backups are stored as `.iosdevicebackup` files. Deleting the file from the location in the filesystem where it was created and restarting Apple Configurator will remove any backups. The **Other** option in the **Restore** menu can then be used to import those `.iosdevicebackup` files into other Apple Configurator clients rather than repeating the step of creating a backup if you have multiple Apple Configurator stations.

There's more...

There are some more points that need to be kept in mind while creating a device backup.

Device activation

Devices can be configured in iTunes, simply using the device and so on. At a minimum, devices should be activated prior to creating the backup so that restored devices are set up and end users do not have to click on the screen a dozen times to activate devices.

Devices will still need to be activated. Therefore, the computer running Apple Configurator should always be able to access the Internet while mass restoring devices.

Naming conventions

As time goes on, you're likely to end up with a lot of different device backups. Therefore, it is a good idea to start with a good naming convention for your backups from day one. Consider using words in the name to indicate what's contained in the backup, and maybe date stamps. For example, you might call a backup `CorpBackground01012013`. Given that we always like having a backup of a freshly installed, otherwise untouched device, that could be `FactoryDefaults01012013`.

Restoring a device backup (Should know)

Once you have a good backup of an iOS device, it's time to restore that backup to another device. At this point, you can also test whether all of the things you think will be there actually are. This can be a somewhat dangerous process, as once we tell Apple Configurator to run the restore process, there is the potential to wipe anything plugged into the USB port of the computer.

Getting ready

The most important thing you can do to prepare for restoring devices is to put your personal devices in your pocket, messenger bag, or backpack. If those devices are plugged in during this exercise, they will be wiped.

Additionally, make sure that the target devices you're restoring the backup made in the previous recipe are wiped clean and therefore have been backed up if need be. The reason we prefer a wiped and not-yet-activated device at this point is to showcase the fact that after restoring through Apple Configurator, the device will not need to go through the setup process.

How to do it...

Preparing a device is a simple process. While configuring the device, we're also going to look at how to configure updates to a newer version of iOS, renaming devices, and erasing devices at the same time.

1. To get started, open Apple Configurator.
2. Click on the **Prepare** button in the top row of icons.
3. In this example, we've configured a traditional base image that can be laid down when devices are turned back in after having been deployed:
    i. Erase the device.
    ii. Update to the latest version of iOS.
    iii. Assign the device a number. Put a factory default (but activated) profile on the devices.

4. It seems like a lot, so let's just go through the fields that were selected and what they can do:

   - **Name**: Renames each device with the name indicated
   - **Number sequentially starting at 1**: If the **Name** field is used, appends a number to the end, starting at the number 1
   - **Supervision**: Enables device supervision, which is covered in the later recipes
   - **iOS**: Allows for selecting a specific version of iOS or simply the latest available
   - **Erase before installing**: Wipes devices before loading a version of iOS (this option requires the iOS field to be set)
   - **Restore**: Choose a backup, created in the *Creating a device backup* recipe
   - **Profiles**: Select one or many profiles (creating and managing profiles is covered thoroughly later)
   - **Apps**: The Apps button along the top of the screen allows you to add .ipa bundles into Apple Configurator (see the later recipes for more on managing apps with Apple Configurator)

5. Once the fields are configured as needed, click on the **Prepare** button.

 Once you click on the **Prepare** button, every iOS device connected to the computer will receive the preparation you have configured. If you don't want personal devices to accidentally get wiped please put them far, far away. The first time you set Apple Configurator to prepare devices, you will get yet another warning about this.

While preparing devices, Apple Configurator fields cannot be altered. The **Prepare** button turns into a **Stop** button, which can be used to go back to the configuration screen and configure devices.

How it works...

After you stop the configuration process, you can customize the environment and start it again quickly and easily. Each time you open Apple Configurator, you will need to configure the environment and start the preparation again.

While in the device preparation (or Supervision) mode, you can configure 30 devices concurrently, although it is a few less if you are also updating the version of iOS at the same time. The old way of restoring devices was to use iTunes, which could only restore one device at a time. Therefore, Apple Configurator is able to manage devices at a much faster rate, tweaked specifically for mass deployment.

There's more...

Along with the advancements with backup creation, there are times when it is not always feasible to do so. However, there are alternatives in backup creation.

iOS 5 versus iOS 6

A device backup created for iOS 5 cannot be restored to a device running iOS 6. This has been consistent with new releases of the iOS operating system. Plan on making new device backups and altering the Apple Configurator workflow each time a new major release of the operating system comes out.

Point releases (for example, iOS 6.1 or 6.2) have never required creating a new backup and so should be fine in this regard.

Backing up Apple Configurator

Once you start getting good data into Apple Configurator, you're not going to want to have to redo all of your work. Additionally, when we get to managing VPP codes with Apple Configurator you're more than likely going to want to back up the database as you don't want to risk losing all the codes. To back up Configurator, please check out Apple's website, `http://support.apple.com/kb/HT5194`.

In the previous set of recipes, we looked at building device backups, updating the OS on devices, renaming devices, and wiping devices. We also noted that if an option or setting that you are trying to configure is available in profiles, then you should configure that option in a profile rather than in a backup or another location. This provides the most granularly manageable environment possible. In this section, we look at what a profile is, how to create a profile, and then some of the things that can be done with profiles once created.

The user experience is perhaps the most important element to building out how you want devices to appear to end users. The best way to craft this experience is using configuration profiles, which fine-tune the device and allow administrators not only to set up policies on devices in the form of profiles, but also to automate the configuration of various services, such as ActiveSync clients for Microsoft Exchange, Calendar clients, and access to shared Contacts.

By approaching imaging iOS devices in a layered and somewhat modular approach, you will have the most flexibility to get devices prepared for users en masse while also not spending a ton of time building out each iteration of how the user experience is crafted for users.

Understanding profiles (Become an expert)

A profile is an XML file, in the property list format. This is the same type of file most commonly associated with managing preferences in OS X. In iOS, a profile, which uses the .mobileconfig extension, manages preferences in iOS and also has the ability to lock preferences in place, by not allowing the profile to be removed. In this recipe, we'll take a .mobileconfig file and view it so that we can see what is going on in the file. Don't worry if you don't have any profiles from other applications, you can skip this recipe and come back to it after you're done with the section.

Getting ready

The only thing you need to have to complete this task is a profile exported into a .mobileconfig file and a copy of TextEdit, which comes with every copy of OS X. If you don't have a profile, create one without any settings or simply perform the rest of the tasks in this book and come back to this one when finished. Alternatively, read this section just to get an understanding of what's in a profile and come back to it.

How to do it...

If you have a profile, provided it isn't encrypted (an option available in iPhone Configuration Utility), you can view it in clear text using the TextEdit application, built into every copy of OS X.

If you double-click on a .mobileconfig file (which again is just a profile) in OS X, then the computer will attempt to install the profile by default. Therefore, to view a profile, follow the given steps:

1. Open TextEdit.
2. Navigate to **File | Open** to browse the file.
3. Once you've browsed to the file, click on the file. Click on the **Open** button.
4. When the file opens, you will see a standard XML structure, but with some strange characters at the top and the bottom of the file. The strange characters are the plain text representation of the signing that Apple Configurator does to the file. At the very bottom of the file, notice that Apple Configurator is referenced, followed by the MAC address of the computer that created the profile.

Scroll down. After the strange characters that make up the digital signature, you'll notice that the file has a standard property list header. This tells applications what's in the file and is in almost every property list. After that, there is a PayloadContent key that has an array of all of the different options that are enabled for the profile. If this profile had a Wi-Fi password on it, you'd see that in clear text.

The profile also has keys at the bottom for a name for the profile (usually the filename), whether the profile can be removed (the **PayloadRemovalDisallowed** key), a unique identifier (the information provided at the time the profile was created, followed by a generated ID to keep two profiles from accidentally occupying the same namespace), a version number, a UUID for the profile, and possibly other information if the profile requires it.

How it works...

No matter which tool is used to create a profile, they will all have the same structure and if the same information is put into them, it should also have a similar makeup. This is because the iOS device (or OS X computer as profiles can be used to configure preferences in OS X) has a built-in interpreter for the profile and expects them to follow certain rules.

Over the years there have been features that weren't supported in graphical interfaces but that were made available in property lists. As such, you can hand create these files, or even use custom scripts to create them. Doing so enables these hidden features, such as the ability to disable the home button before App Lock mode was introduced.

These days, there's very little reason to create a profile manually. You can create one using iPhone Configuration Utility, Apple Configurator, Profile Manager (built into `Server.app` in Lion and above), and a variety of third-party MDM utilities. Profiles, once created, can then be ported between systems using the `.mobileconfig` files and installed on devices. When installing `.mobileconfig` files, you can use a web server, e-mail, Apple Configurator, or even use an MDM server to enforce the policies without a static profile.

There's more...

For more information on what Apple Configurator is doing under the hood, check out `http://krypted.com/iphone/talking-a-look-under-apple-configurators-hood`.

Profiles and OS X

Many profiles can be installed on iOS or OS X. Installing a profile on an OS X computer is done by simply double-clicking on a profile. Once installed, you can then view what the profile does by clicking on the profile and viewing the details from the **Profiles System Preference** pane.

For example, the details of the profile we just looked at in this task can be seen in the following screenshot:

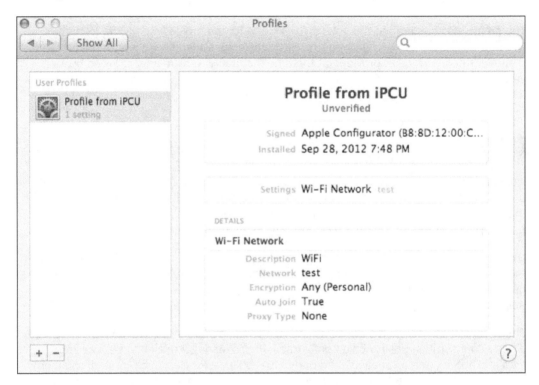

Viewing profiles from iOS

The contents of a profile can also be viewed in iOS. To do so, open the **Settings** app and then click on **General** and scroll down until you see **Profile**. Click on **Profile** and then on the specific profile whose contents you'd like to see. The following screenshot shows the payloads configured for the profile viewed previously in this task:

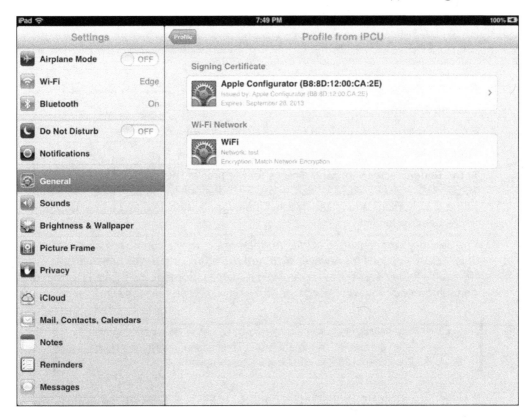

Provided the profile is removable, simply click on the **Remove** button to delete it. If there is no **Remove** button, then the profile cannot be removed.

Building a profile (Must know)

Profiles are very powerful and can do a variety of tasks. The most basic, and probably one of the most used tasks, is to join a wireless network. In this task, we'll look at configuring this basic profile and then deploying that profile to a device.

Getting ready

Before configuring a profile that provides access to a Wi-Fi network, you should first have a Wi-Fi network up and running and ready. If the network is 802.1x (Network Access Control or Certificate-based Authentication), then you should also have a certificate or other requirements to join the network on hand to be added to the profile prior to getting the profile configured.

How to do it...

Once the wireless network is ready, follow the given steps:

1. Open Apple Configurator.

2. Click on **Prepare**.

3. From the main screen, click on the plus sign to create a new profile.

4. From the list of options, click on **Create New Profile**.

5. At the **General** screen, provide a name for the profile. This is often something like `Wireless Profile` or `802.1x Profile`. Additionally, the profile can have the name of the organization filled in using the **Organization** field and a brief description in the **Description** field.

6. The **Security** field is used to configure whether the profile can be removed. This includes options for **Always**, **With Authorization**, and **Never**, which allow the profile to be removed, to be removed if the password for the profile is provided, and to never be removed (except for with a device reset) respectively.

 The only type of profile that cannot be set to **Never** be removable is an automatic enrolment profile, discussed later in this book. Enrollment profiles must always be removable.

7. Fields that initially say **[required]** and with a red circle with an arrow are required and fields that say **[optional]** are not.

 You cannot save the profile until you configure at least one more payload. The payloads are listed below the **General** entry in the sidebar of the profile popover screen.

8. Click on **Wi-Fi** to configure the wireless networks the iOS device will automatically join. Here, click on **Configure** to enable the payload. At the Wi-Fi screen you have the following options:

   ❑ **Plus (+) and minus (-) buttons**: Add additional wireless networks the iOS device will join

   ❑ **Service Set Identifier (SSID)**: Defines the wireless network the iOS device will join

   ❑ **Hidden Network**: If the SSID is suppressed, use this option

- ❑ **Auto Join**: If the device should join the network automatically without prompting end users, check this box

- ❑ **Proxy Setup**: Allows administrators to define the path to a PAC file (using the **Automatic** option) or manually enter profile information (using the **Manual** option)

- ❑ **Security Type**: Set to **WEP**, **WPA / WPA2**, **Any (Personal)** networks, which simply use a password or WEP Enterprise, **WPA / WPA2 Enterprise** or **Any (Enterprise)**, which require a second factor of authentication (802.1x)

- ❑ **Password**: The password to join the WEP, WPA, or WPA2 network

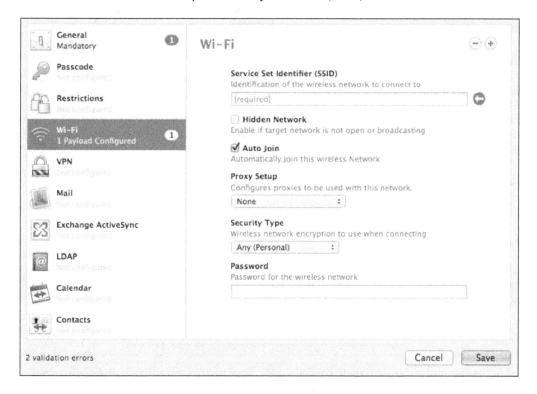

9. Configure the wireless network as is appropriate and click on **Save** to save the profile. We don't go through all of the options in this book for 802.1x as most will require input from the administrators of these types of wireless networks.

10. Once the profile is created, click on **Save** to save the profile. Click on the checkbox for the profile to enable it (multiple profiles can be enabled concurrently).

11. Clicking on **Prepare** or **Refresh** (under **Supervision**) enables the profile for devices that are then plugged in.

Once the installation of a profile begins, someone will need to accept the profile on the devices the profile is being installed on. Finally, if any profiles automatically enroll devices into SCEP servers or MDM servers, the server in which the device is being enrolled must be online at the time of enrollment.

How it works...

Profiles can be installed as a unique step or as part of a larger workflow where devices are being updated, getting backups restored to them, erased, and even having apps installed. The profile installation itself requires interaction with the device as Apple has made a decision that rather than have policies enforced without an end user's choice in the matter, profiles must be accepted by end users. MDM servers can make changes without devices accepting each change because doing so is trusted by the enrolment profile.

Once a device accepts a profile, the profile can easily be removed using the **Remove** button, provided the profile is removable. If using an MDM server, then a few other items should be installed other than the automated enrolment profile and a Wi-Fi network so the device can actually reach the MDM server. However, if no MDM server is available then there are a number of options available to administrators for controlling devices; however, updating devices must then be done physically by connecting via USB.

There's more...

Profiles in iOS work much the same as profiles in OS X, just without the manual, programmatic interfaces. Obviously, not all options are supported in both; however, one should understand each. For more information on processing profiles in OS X, check out `http://krypted.com/iphone/profile-manager-and-profiles`.

Empty fields

Apple Configurator has the ability to configure a number of different settings. But some might not be known to administrators. These are primarily password fields. In the event that you do not know a username or a password, then fields can be left blank and end users will be prompted for whatever credentials are missing at the time the profile is installed.

Exploring all profiles (Should know)

In the previous recipe, we defined a wireless network that devices automatically join once the profile is installed. In this task, we're going to look at all of the other features available to Apple Configurator administrators. These include:

▶ Configuring policies

▶ Passcode restrictions

▶ Microsoft Exchange connectivity, and more

Each of the options that is enabled is considered an additional payload installed by the profile and appears in the description when a profile is viewed on the devices of end users. These payloads, if an MDM server is available, should usually be installed by MDM.

But most environments do not have an MDM solution in place. Therefore, your task is to go through each available payload, thus educating yourself on what is possible with regards to centralized profile management.

Getting ready

Because we created a payload in the previous task, we're going to build on the work that was already performed. Therefore, you should have a payload for Wi-Fi already created prior to starting this task.

How to do it...

1. Open the previously created payload (or create a new one and fill in the general information).

2. For each payload that you are going to configure, click on the payload title in the Apple Configurator sidebar.

3. Click on the **Configure** button.

   We'll start with the Passcode payload, which defines the type of PIN code that must be used on devices.

4. Click on the **Passcode** payload in the Apple Configurator sidebar.

5. Click on **Configure** to see the options available in the Passcode payload. These options along with their descriptions can be seen in the following screenshot:

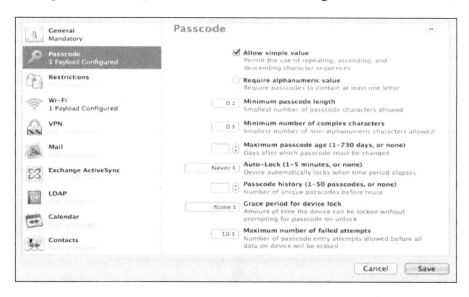

6. Next, click on **Restrictions**. The Restrictions payload is used to disable features of iOS. The controls are set in three different sections, as follows:

  ❑ **Functionality**: The **Functionality** section includes the following options:

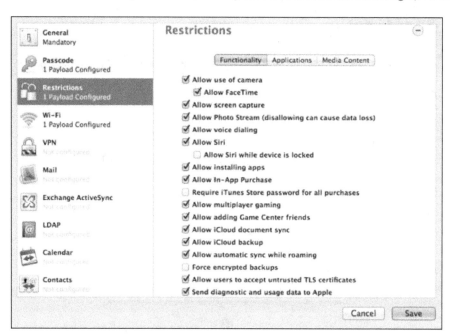

Allow use of camera: Uncheck this option to disable both the front facing camera and rear facing camera on the device. Photos can still be used but the cameras no longer operate.

Allow FaceTime: Uncheck this option to disable the FaceTime application.

Allow screen capture: Uncheck this option to disable the ability to make screenshots (press and hold menu, then Sleep/Wake if you haven't done this before).

Allow Photo Stream (disallowing can cause data loss): Uncheck this option to disable the Photo Stream feature from iCloud. If you don't have an iCloud account, there's no need to do so.

Allow voice dialing: Uncheck this option to disable the voice dial feature.

Allow Siri: Uncheck this option to disable voice activated commands using Siri.

Allow Siri while device is locked: Leave Siri enabled, except when the device is locked (automatically enabled when Siri is disabled).

Allow installing apps: Uncheck this option to disable the ability to install apps (note, if you disable this option, then you as the administrator cannot install apps either).

Allow In-App Purchase: Uncheck this option to disable the ability for any app to perform an in-app purchase (for example, unlocking those extra levels in Angry Birds).

Require iTunes Store password for all purchases: Forces the Apple ID for the iTunes Store account to be entered, along with a password for that account, each time an app is purchased.

Allow multiplayer gaming: Uncheck this option to disable any apps that leverage the multiplayer gaming API.

Allow adding Game Center friends: Uncheck this option to disable adding friends in Game Center (note, this does not disable Game Center itself).

Allow iCloud document sync: Disable the ability to synchronize documents with iCloud.

Allow iCloud backup: Disable the ability to back data up on devices through iCloud.

Allow automatic sync while roaming: Disable synchronization while the device's antenna is roaming.

Force encrypted backups: Forces backups of devices to be encrypted in iTunes.

> **Allow users to accept untrusted TLS certificates**: When checked, users can only access certificates that are trusted.

> **Send diagnostic and usage data to Apple**: Disable the ability to send diagnostic data to Apple.

❑ **Applications**: The **Applications** section includes the following options:

> **Allow use of YouTube**: Uncheck this option to disable the YouTube app (which then no longer appears on the device and disables YouTube access from within Safari).

> **Allow use of iTunes Store**: Uncheck this option to disable the App Store app (and therefore the ability to install apps).

> **Allow use of Safari**: When unchecked, this option disables the Safari app. Third-party web browsers can still be used.

> **Enable autofill**: When unchecked, this option disables the ability to use stored data to automatically fill forms on devices.

> **Force fraud warning**: When checked, this option forces the fraud warning screen (otherwise it can be disabled).

> **Enable JavaScript**: When unchecked, this option disables the ability to use JavaScript.

> **Block pop-ups**: When checked, this option disables site pop-ups.

> **Accept Cookies**: When unchecked, this option disables the ability for the device to accept cookies from websites.

❑ **Media Content**: The **Media Content** section includes the following sections:

> **Ratings region**: Automatically configures regions for ratings use.

> > **Allow content ratings**: This further has the following options:

> > **Movies**: Disables access to movies based on their ratings.

> > **TV Shows**: Disables access to television shows based on their ratings.

> > **Apps**: Restricts access to apps based on their ratings.

> **Allow explicit music & podcasts**: Disable the ability to access music or podcasts that contain explicit content.

7. Next, click on **Virtual Private Network (VPN)**. A VPN server allows users to connect to services on the local network as though they were on the network over untrusted networks. The VPN payload is used to automatically configure VPN connections. Multiple accounts can be configured. To enable VPN, use the following options:

    ❑ **Connection Name**: A name for the VPN network.

- ❑ **Connection Type**: The protocol or vendor of the VPN endpoint, including IPSEC, L2TP, and PPTP are the most common protocols as well as vendor-specific connections in Cisco AnyConnect, Juniper SSL, F5 SSL, SonicWALL Mobile Connect, and non-vendor specific Custom SSL.

- ❑ **Server**: The host name or IP address of the server.

- ❑ **Account**: A valid username with access to the VPN service.

- ❑ **User Authentication**: Most environments will use a password to connect, although RSA SecurID is supported as well.

- ❑ **Shared Secret**: The second factor for security, a shared secret shared by users, is not required for PPTP but is for most other types of connections.

- ❑ **Send All Traffic**: Uses the VPN for all traffic, not just that local to the VPN network. For example, when checked, all web traffic goes through the VPN tunnel, even if not destined for a web server on the VPN. When disabled, it sends traffic destined for public networks over the WAN interface of the local router.

- ❑ **Proxy Setup**: Defines proxy server connections, either using automatic (through a PAC file) or manual, where each entry for proxy communications is defined separately and manually.

8. Once you have defined the appropriate VPN information, click on **Mail**.

 Leaving a field blank for these subsequent payloads prompts users to input information. For example, leaving the **Account** field blank will prompt users for the account name when the profile is installed.

9. The Mail payload defines accounts to connect to mail services. Here, connections to POP and IMAP servers can be defined. Exchange accounts should be defined in the Exchange ActiveSync payload, which we will cover next. Click on **Configure** to set up a mail account and then provide the following information about the account(s) being defined:

- ❑ **Account Description**: A name that helps the user of the device remember which account this is.

- ❑ **Account Type**: This tells whether the account will be a POP or an IMAP account. POP removes mail from the server whereas IMAP synchronizes mail to the server.

- ❑ **User Display Name**: The name shown to those who receive e-mail messages from the sender.

- ❑ **Email Address**: The e-mail address for the account being set up.

❑ **Do not allow user to move messages from this account**: Disables the ability to move mail from one account to another.

❑ **Use Only in Mail**: Only allows outgoing mail to go through the mail app rather than through a third-party apps connection to the mail API.

❑ **Enable S/MIME**: Enables per-message encryption and decryption. Requires a certificate to be installed as well, done with the Credentials payload.

❑ **Incoming Mail**: The following information is needed while configuring the incoming mail:

> **Mail Server and Port**: The server hostname or IP address with a second field for the port number (changes based on the protocol and whether SSL is supported).
>
> **User Name**: The user's account name on the server (can be left blank to prompt the user at the time the account is created).
>
> **Authentication Type**: Most environments use password authentication, although some (as per the administrator of the server usually) use MD5, NTLM, or HTTP MD5 Digest, all supported by the payload.
>
> **Password**: The user's password on the server (can also be left blank to prompt the user at the time the account is created).
>
> **Use SSL**: Enables SSL certificates for the connection. These certificates need to be installed in the credentials payload and then appear when the checkbox is checked.

❑ **Outgoing Mail**: The following information is needed while configuring the outgoing mail:

> **Mail Server and Port**: The server hostname or IP address with a second field for the port number (changes based on the protocol and whether SSL is supported).
>
> **User Name**: The user's account name on the server (can be left blank to prompt the user at the time the account is created).
>
> **Authentication Type**: Most environments use password authentication, although some (as per the administrator of the server usually) use MD5, NTLM, or HTTP MD5 Digest, all supported by the payload.
>
> **Password**: The user's password on the server (can also be left blank to prompt the user at the time the account is created).

> **Outgoing password same as incoming**: Automatically sets the password for the outgoing (SMTP) account to be the same as the incoming account's password.
>
> **Use SSL**: Enables SSL certificates for the connection. These certificates need to be installed in the Credentials payload and then appear when the checkbox is checked.

10. Next, click on **Exchange ActiveSync** to configure the Exchange ActiveSync payload. This payload is specifically designed to connect to servers that run Microsoft Exchange Server 2007 or later or servers that have support for the ActiveSync protocol (such as Google Apps). Click on **Configure** to set up an account and then provide the following information, as shown in the screenshot:

    ❑ **Account Description**: A name for the account that is easy for the end user to remember (does not need to match any information on the server).

    ❑ **Exchange ActiveSync Host**: The name or IP address of the Exchange ActiveSync server (usually a CAS role within the Exchange organization).

    ❑ **Use SSL**: Enables SSL certificates for the connection. These certificates need to be installed in the Credentials payload and then appear when the checkbox is checked.

    ❑ **Domain**: The domain name (for example, `yourdomainname.com`).

    ❑ **User**: The user's account name on the server (can be left blank to prompt the user at the time the account is created).

    ❑ **Email Address**: The e-mail address for the Exchange account.

    ❑ **Password**: The user's password on the server (can also be left blank to prompt the user at the time the account is created).

    ❑ **Past Days of Mail to Sync**: The history of mail being synchronized to the device.

    ❑ **Authentication Credential**: Allows for the using of a SCEP server to pull down SSL information.

    ❑ **Do not allow user to move messages from this account**: Disables the ability to move mail between e-mail accounts (for example, putting a message in the folder of a different e-mail account.

    ❑ **Use Only in Mail**: Disables the ability to use SMTP for this e-mail account by another app other than the Mail app.

      ❏   **Enable S/MIME**: Enables encrypting outgoing mail through S/MIME. Requires a certificate to be selected as well.

11. Next, click on the **LDAP** payload, used for looking up contacts stored in an LDAP server. This is how you would access contacts stored in Open Directory if the LDAP gateway feature is enabled on an OS X server. To configure the LDAP payload, click on **Continue** and then provide the following information:

      ❏   **Account Description**: A name for the account that is easy for the end user to remember (does not need to match any information on the server).

      ❏   **Account Username**: The user's account name on the server (can be left blank to prompt the user at the time the account is created).

      ❏   **Account Password**: The user's password on the server (can also be left blank to prompt the user at the time the account is created).

      ❏   **Account Hostname**: The name or IP address of the LDAP server.

      ❏   **Use SSL**: Enables SSL certificates for the connection. These certificates need to be installed in the Credentials payload and then appear when the checkbox is checked.

❏ **Search Settings**: Allows for the placing of a search base into the configuration (see the LDAP administrator for information regarding whether or not this is necessary).

12. The Calendar payload configures access to CalDAV servers. If you use Exchange calendaring, this is configured with the Exchange ActiveSync payload instead. If you use a CalDAV server though (as is common with OS X Server environments), click on **Configure** and then provide the following information:

❏ **Account Description**: A name for the account that is easy for the end user to remember (does not need to match any information on the server).

❏ **Account Hostname and Port**: The name or IP address of the CalDAV server. Also provide a custom port number if the port has been changed from the default setting.

❏ **Principal URL**: The URL in the server to the account. This should automatically fill in for each device based on username.

❏ **Account Username**: The user's account name on the server (can be left blank to prompt the user at the time the account is created).

❏ **Account Password**: The user's password on the server (can also be left blank to prompt the user at the time the account is created).

❏ **Use SSL**: Enables SSL certificates for the connection. These certificates need to be installed in the Credentials payload and then appear when the checkbox is checked.

13. The Contacts payload configures a CardDAV client, common in OS X Server hosted groupware environments. To configure the CardDAV client, click on the **CardDAV** payload and then click on **Configure**. Once prompted, provide the following information:

❏ **Account Description**: A name for the account that is easy for the end user to remember (does not need to match any information on the server).

❏ **Account Hostname and Port**: The name or IP address of the CardDAV server. Also provides a custom port number if the port has been changed from the default setting.

❏ **Principal URL**: The URL in the server to the account. This should automatically fill in for each device based on username.

❏ **Account Username**: The user's account name on the server (can be left blank to prompt the user at the time the account is created).

❏ **Account Password**: The user's password on the server (can also be left blank to prompt the user at the time the account is created).

❏ **Use SSL**: Enables SSL certificates for the connection. These certificates need to be installed in the Credentials payload and then appear when the checkbox is checked.

14. Next, click on the **Subscribed Calendars** payload. Subscribed Calendars are a means of accessing publicly posted calendars. The Subscribed Calendars payload configures access to these calendars (which are usually ICA files). Click on **Configure** to begin the configuration of the payload. The options to set up Subscribed Calendars are as follows:

   ❑ **Description**: The name that will appear in the calendar app for each instance of a shared calendar.

   ❑ **URL**: The address of the ICA file that the instance is subscribing to.

   ❑ **Username**: The user's account name on the server (can be left blank to prompt the user at the time the account is created).

   ❑ **Password**: The user's password on the server (can also be left blank to prompt the user at the time the account is created).

   ❑ **Use SSL**: Enables SSL certificates for the connection. These certificates need to be installed in the Credentials payload and then appear when the checkbox is checked.

Web clips are links that appear on an iOS device as though they are an app. You can configure multiple payloads of web clips to place multiple links on target devices. This is commonly used to send a link to enrol into an MDM server, put the organization's official site on each device, a link to the course management software in schools, or maybe a link to the company' document repository.

15. Configure the Web Clips payload by clicking on **Web Clips** and then on the **Configure** button. Then provide the following information for each site:

   ❑ **Label**: The name that appears on the home screen under the badge.

   ❑ **URL**: The address of the site.

   ❑ **Removable**: Disables the ability to remove a web clip.

   ❑ **Icon**: Allows administrators to upload an icon rather than using the one that appears in the address bar of the web browser.

   ❑ **Precomposed Icon**: iOS rounds corners of app badges and puts a horizon effect on badges. This option automatically configures the app badge for what was uploaded rather than applying these effects.

   ❑ **Full Screen**: Hides the address bar when the page is opened, having the effect that the website appears as though it were an app in some cases.

16. The Credentials payload is used to automatically populate the iOS device with a certificate or multiple certificates. To configure this payload, first have the certificates on hand and ready to import. When you click on the **Configure** button, you will be prompted to import the certificates immediately. Once imported, the certificates can be used by other payloads as well.

17. The SCEP payload automatically enrolls devices into an **SCEP (Simple Certificate Enrollment Protocol**) server. SCEP servers are handy as they allow administrators to automatically revoke certificates. Work with your SCEP systems administrator to configure this payload as it's very specific to each environment where SCEP is leveraged.

18. The APN payload is used to configure connections to an Apple Push Notification server. This should be done under the watchful eye of an APN administrator. Both the SCEP and APN payloads require the services to be accessible at the time the payload is installed.

19. Once payloads are configured as intended, click on the **Save** button to save any changes to the profile. Install the profile on devices to test that the settings are interpreted by iOS as intended.

One thing to be careful of with regard to making multiple profiles is that each profile needs to be accepted on devices. This means that when imaging a large number of devices you will not want to put a different payload into each profile; otherwise you'll spend a lot of time clicking on **Accept** and **Done** buttons!

How it works...

Each payload enabled adds data into the XML structure of the `.mobileconfig` file. Each option you enable toggles or fills in a setting of that same file. When the file is applied on the device, the configuration options are applied. If the profile is removable, then removing the profile also removes any of the data that came with the configuration. For example, if mail is configured with a profile that also has restrictions on it, removing the profile with the restrictions on it also ends up removing the mail that was downloaded with the profile.

There's more...

There are certain activities which can be performed while working with payload entries.

Multiple instances and removing payload entries

Each payload has the ability to have multiple instances of settings (except **Passcode**, **Restrictions**, and **APN**). This means that you can have multiple mail accounts, multiple VPN connections, multiple Wi-Fi networks, and so on. In order to make additions to any payload, click on the plus sign button [**+**] in the upper right-hand corner of the payload screen. In order to remove one, click on the minus sign button [**–**]. If you remove the last instance of the payload declaration, you will be left with the **Configure** button, meaning that the payload is not being configured.

Exporting profiles (Must know)

A lot of work can go into building profiles. Rather than building profiles in multiple programs, they can be exported into `.mobileconfig` files. It's also important to be able to export profiles as you may choose to distribute those profiles through mail or a web portal and possibly even install profiles in OS X rather than considering profiles to be specific to iOS-based devices.

In this task, we're going to take the profile that we created previously in this book and export it into a file on the desktop of our computer.

Getting ready

Before exporting the profile, it should be complete. If using mail or a web portal to distribute profiles, once they're distributed there will be no changing of the payload without uninstalling profiles and installing new ones. If moving to a different Apple Configurator station, though, you will have the opportunity to augment the profile once moved.

How to do it...

To export a profile, follow the given steps:

1. Open Apple Configurator.

2. Click on **Prepare** in the top row of icons to see the main **Preparation** screen (shown in the following screenshot).

3. At the **Save As** screen, choose a name for the profile being exported. The name that appears in Apple Configurator is used by default, but is easily changed.

4. Choose the location for the profile in the **Where:** field.

5. Choose whether or not to add a digital signature to the profile, which can be used to verify authenticity, using the **Sign Configuration Profile** checkbox. Click on **Save** to export the profile into a `.mobileconfig` file.

How it works...

Once exported, the profile can be viewed using a standard text editor, as shown in the *Viewing profiles from iOS* section. The `.mobileconfig` files that make up the profile can then be moved and copied between computers.

There's more...

Some of the profiles are often accompanied by additional information which authenticates the identity of the user.

Signatures

The signature that is applied to a profile when choosing to sign them allows administrators and end users to verify the authenticity of a profile prior to installing the profile. However, there are no prompts in Apple Configurator when installing profiles. Therefore, you can install the profile on OS X prior to installing it in Apple Configurator in order to validate that the profile is what it claims to be.

Creating auto enrollment profiles (Become an expert)

Apple Configurator can create a profile that is used to enroll tens or thousands of devices into an MDM solution. Doing so provides centralized management en masse while minimizing the time it requires to configure devices. This is how most environments are going to mass deploy iOS devices that will be enrolled into an MDM service.

But it is worth noting that when using an automated enrolment profile as opposed to a web clip that points users at an enrolment web page, you will miss out on one thing: you will not know which device is in which user's hands. There are ways to obtain that information, such as the name of the device or the serial that's likely tracked along with which staff member has a device, but the MDM solution isn't likely to associate devices with users automatically without some link that tells users who has which device.

Getting ready

Apple Configurator is not a tool for over-the-air configurations of devices. But it can help to get devices enrolled provided that they can access an MDM solution, such as Apple's Profile Manager or third-party solutions such as AirWatch or Casper MDM. Each of the third-party solutions should have a unique way of enrolling devices. Therefore, make sure to check with your vendor prior to creating an enrolment profile, as this task is meant to showcase the ability.

Before getting started, make sure that devices can log into the wireless network (often done through the use of a profile) and make sure that once logged into a wireless network, devices can access a well functioning MDM server.

How to do it...

To download an enrollment profile from JAMF's Casper MDM, follow these steps:

1. First log in to the web interface of the JSS, seen in the following screenshot:

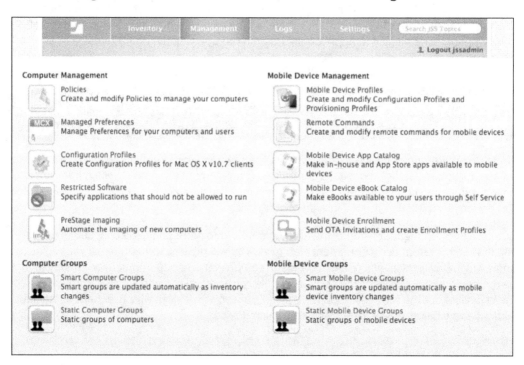

2. Click on the link for **Mobile Device Enrollment** on the **Mobile Device Enrollment Invitations** screen.

3. Click on the **Enrollment Profiles** tab. On the **Enrollment Profiles** screen, click on **Download** for the appropriate profile (for most environments there should only be one as shown in the following screenshot):

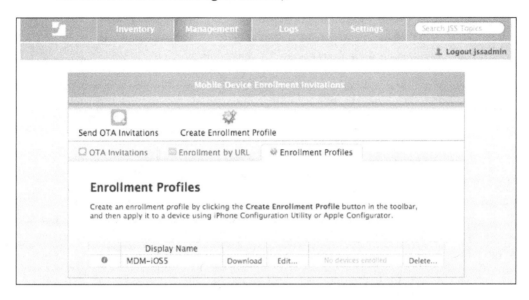

4. Once the profile is downloaded, it will automatically attempt to enroll the computer you are downloading it from in the **Profiles System Preferences** pane. Click on **Cancel** to keep the profile from installing. Click on the downloads link in Safari.

5. Click on the magnifying glass icon to see the `.mobileconfig` file.

6. You have now downloaded the `.mobileconfig` file that will enroll devices into Casper MDM. To deploy the profile through Apple Configurator, open Apple Configurator on the client computer. Click on **Prepare** in the row of icons along the top of the screen. Drag the profile (by default currently called `MDM-iOS5.mobileconfig`) from the Finder into the list of **Profiles**. The profile then appears in Apple Configurator.

7. Check the box for the newly added profile to add it to any workflow.

8. The subsequent screen shows when devices are being configured. Here, dock the device to receive the profile (note, all docked iOS devices are going to be configured with this profile).

9. Now from the device, once the profile is installing on the device, click on the **Install** button.

10. Click on **Install** on the device again to complete the installation.

11. Once the profile is installed, click on **Done**.

To unenroll from MDM, simply remove the profiles by clicking on **Profiles** and then clicking on the **Remove** button. According to the MDM API, a user can elect to remove their device from management at any point, so expect this will happen occasionally, even if only by accident.

How it works...

Once the enrollment profile and corresponding trust profile is installed on each iOS device, the MDM server that the device is enrolled in will be able to manage that device remotely. Management starts with an Apple Push Notification Service each time a change is made as well as for regular check-ins. This push notification tells the device to check in with the server. When the device checks in, the server provides any payloads to the device.

Payloads can include any of the options we've covered that are otherwise configured with profiles. However, centralized management using an MDM solution allows for over-the-air changes to profiles, rather than waiting for devices to check back in. This allows for the most highly configurable and quickly changed solution available.

Even if using an MDM solution, though, installing profiles through Apple Configurator still plays an integral part in managing iOS devices. The most notable payloads being to set up a Wi-Fi network to establish a network connection to an MDM server and then to install the automatic enrolment profile.

There's more...

Let's take a look at what we should do in case we don't have an MDM provider.

Mobile Device Management providers

If you do not yet have an MDM provider, consider checking out the wiki at `http://enterpriseios.com/wiki/Comparison_MDM_Providers`, which contains a comparison of each of the vendors currently providing device management for iOS. Here, you can find out which solutions support the various options your organization considers important and maybe even find out about products you haven't yet heard of!

iOS 6 is a great device, out of the box. It can access e-mail, leverage iMessages to communicate with friends, get you anywhere in the world you need to go, share calendars, access contacts, keep up on scores with the web browser, and pretty much live the dream. But the real power in iOS is the wealth of games, business productivity, student learning, and personal productivity apps available on the App Store. Without these apps and the extent that the developer community has grown, it is arguable that while great devices, the iOS family would not be so entrenched in schools, enterprises, non-profits, and small businesses around the globe.

When dealing with apps on a small scale (for example, for my iPhone at home), little is needed; an Internet connection, a valid Apple ID, and a credit card. But when configuring a large number of iOS devices, more complex situations come up. For example, you can't give students credit card access to buy the apps they need on devices. Companies need to be able to centrally manage the distribution of apps and therefore the data within them and of course, you need users to know exactly which apps they should have.

In this section, we'll look at leveraging the Volume Purchasing Program from Apple in order to purchase apps en masse and then look at how to distribute those applications through Apple Configurator.

Purchasing applications through the VPP (Should know)

The **Volume Purchase Program** (**VPP**) is available to users in Australia, Canada, France, Germany, Italy, Japan, New Zealand, Spain, the United Kingdom, and the United States. The VPP allows administrators to buy gift codes to purchase applications en masse. There are two VPP programs:

- Education customers
- Business customers

The two VPP programs are similar. Administrators receive a spreadsheet of codes after providing credit card information and purchasing apps. You can buy thousands of codes concurrently and they must be used by your organization.

Getting ready

To get started with the VPP, first create an account. Apple's education customers can sign up for the VPP using `http://www.apple.com/education/volume-purchase-program`. For businesses, sign up for the Volume Purchasing Program using `http://www.apple.com/business/vpp`. Once you have signed up for the program, provide payment information and log in at the portal to make purchases.

How to do it...

Once you have signed up, follow these steps:

1. Go to `https://vpp.itunes.apple.com`.

2. Log into the portal.

3. At the main page, search for an app.

4. At the results page, verify that you are purchasing the correct app. Enter the number of the app that you would like to purchase.

5. Click on the **Continue** button as seen in the following screenshot:

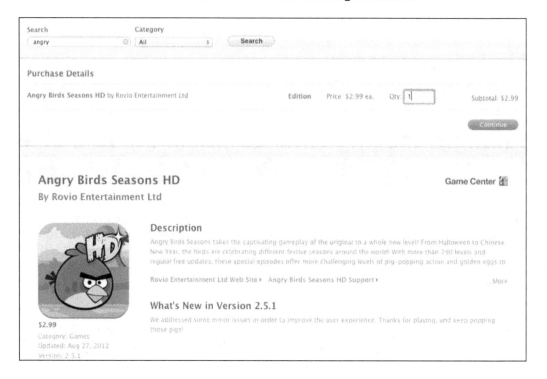

6. The **Purchase Details** screen then displays the number of codes and licenses for the transaction.

7. Click on **Buy** to complete the transaction. The order is then processed and after a few minutes you will see a link for **Download Spreadsheet**.

8. Click on the link to download the VPP spreadsheet, which will have all the access codes you need, as can be seen in the following screenshot:

Volume Purchase Codes						
Order ID	MH3159YQ69					
Product	Angry Birds Seasons HD, v2.5.1					
Purchaser	Charles Edge <iphone@318.com>					
Codes Purchased	1					
Codes Redeemed	0					
Codes Remaining	1					
Code	Code Redemption Link					
69A6WTJPE769	https://buy.itunes.apple.com/WebObjects/MZFinance.woa/wa/freeProductCodeWizard?code=69A6WTJPE769					

You can use the links to directly purchase apps, although for these we are more than likely going to wait and use them in the next task.

How it works...

The spreadsheet can then be imported into Apple Configurator or an MDM tool. When a device opens the link provided via the VPP code, the user is prompted to accept the VPP code and the license that the VPP code represents is transferred to the Apple ID of the user logged into the device.

There's more...

Most countries have access to the VPP program, but there are always exceptions.

Countries without VPP

There are a lot of countries that do not yet have access to the VPP program. Because a VPP code is basically a gift code, you can purchase an app from iTunes and use the code in the app to build a VPP spreadsheet. When doing so, simply replace the 12-digit code in a template spreadsheet with the 12-digit code from the gift code. This is pretty labor-intensive but still allows for administrators in countries where the VPP program is not available to leverage VPP-based technology. One thing to look out for though is that content can only be redeemed in the country it was purchased. So don't plan on giving a bunch of codes to a bunch of users in another country!

Importing applications (Should know)

Once you have VPP codes, apps need to be imported into Apple Configurator in order to use them. Doing so requires downloading each app from the iOS App Store (this will use one of your codes) and then importing it into Apple Configurator. Once imported, VPP codes need to be applied to each app so it can be distributed to devices. This process is covered in this task.

Getting ready

Before importing apps into Apple Configurator it is important that you make sure you're importing the right number of apps into each Apple computer that runs Apple Configurator. For example, if you will be using five workstations to prepare 1,000 devices for users, you would likely import 200 into each one. Or if you have four carts on wheels managing 100 devices evenly distributed between the carts, you would import 25 into the Apple Configurator workstation that goes with each of the carts.

You should also have completed the previous task, where we obtain VPP codes for use with Apple Configurator.

How to do it...

To get started, follow the given steps:

1. Take the link provided in the previous recipe and paste it into Safari (or in a browser of your choice).

2. iTunes automatically opens and prompts you for an Apple ID and password. Provide the appropriate information. This account will then own that license of the software and be able to download the app.

3. When prompted that iTunes is downloading the app, wait for the download to complete.

4. Once downloaded, click on **Apps** in the iTunes sidebar.

5. Locate the app that was just purchased, shown in the following screenshot.

6. Right-click on the app.

 Select **Show** in Finder. The `ipa` bundle for the app then appears in the Finder (by default the Apps are in the `~/Music/iTunes/Mobile Applications` directory). The name of the `.ipa` file sometimes has nothing to do with the name of the app. Use the **Get Info** screen of each app to determine the correct name of the `.ipa` file to be downloaded.

7. Drag the app from the Finder into the **Apps** section of Apple Configurator. You are then prompted again for an Apple ID.

8. If the app doesn't cost money on the App Store, then Apple Configurator will automatically make it available for use. If the app costs money then the App has a caution symbol, as shown in the following screenshot:

For apps that cost money, you can also click on the caution symbol to insert VPP codes. This can be done by simply dragging the VPP code spreadsheet obtained in the previous task or by typing codes manually.

How it works...

The VPP codes imported are immediately marked as used in the iOS App Store. Therefore, before dragging codes in it is important to make sure you want as many as you're dragging in to be used by each Apple Configurator station. These codes are then also marked with the Apple ID of the account used to import them. Therefore, updating apps require that Apple ID for future use.

There's more...

Lots of apps are imported on an Apple computer, but what is equally important is managing them efficiently.

Managing the VPP code spreadsheet

A VPP code spreadsheet can easily be split into multiple parts. Doing so requires creating a separate spreadsheet and copying the header portion of the one Apple provides into the new one. Then, alter the number of codes indicated in the spreadsheet and cut that many rows from the bottom of the original. For example, this allows you to take 100 codes and turn them into two spreadsheets of 50 or five of 20. Each can then be imported into Apple Configurator independently.

Deploying applications on prepared devices (Become an expert)

There are two ways to deploy apps through Apple Configurator. The first, which we cover in this recipe, is to simply place the app on the device. This is done in the **Prepare** mode and the app is never available for re-use. When distributing apps in this manner, a VPP code is used each time a device is prepared. The second, which we cover in the *Deploying applications on managed devices (Become an expert)* recipe, is to supervise a device. When supervising devices, the app code is returned to Apple Configurator when the device is checked back in. This allows you to repurpose codes to devices without the need to be concerned about backing up Apple Configurator.

Getting ready

Pushing an app to a device through preparation allows administrators to distribute apps quickly. However, once an app is pushed to a device, the code is no longer usable. Therefore, make sure that you really want to do this before proceeding. As we discussed in the earlier recipes, you can prepare or supervise devices. However, if you supervise, while you have more flexibility with app and deployment, you lose the ability to ever plug devices into iTunes.

Before placing an app on a device, you also need that app to appear in Apple Configurator. Therefore, make sure to have followed along with previous recipes prior to attempting this one.

How to do it...

1. Once an application has been imported into Apple Configurator, it can be installed on iOS devices. We're going to step through completing an app installation. We're not going to do any reformatting or anything of that sort as a part of this task. In your environment, you may choose to do the app deployment alongside the options defined in **Settings**, including policies, wiping devices, and so on; however, this is not required. Click on **Prepare** in the top row of icons and then click on **Apps** in the second row.

2. Check the box for each app you would like to deploy on devices.

3. Click on the **Prepare** button.

4. Once Apple Configurator is in the preparation mode, plug in a device (or devices).

5. The device then installs the app.

Free apps can also be installed this way, as seen using the iBooks application. Each time a paid app is installed, the counter for available licenses will be reduced by one. As there is no counter for free apps, they will remain unchanged.

How it works...

Apps are just `.ipa` bundles (or a collection of files saved into the `.ipa` format). The `.ipa` file installs on a device simply enough and can actually be placed on a device without the **Digital Rights Management** (**DRM**) side of the license covered. However, when no DRM information is found, the app will not open on the devices. Apple Configurator can handle DRM by showing the app code number and decrementing the number down by one each time a code is used up.

There's more...

Apps are why iOS is such a popular operating system. The variety of apps and the wealth of information available through those apps is above and beyond what was available in the Great Library of Alexandria. Search for anything you need and we're sure you'll be pleasantly surprised by what you find.

Apple IDs

When an app is imported into Apple Configurator, the Apple ID that purchased the app must be supplied. While there is a chance that the app can install, even though the Apple ID is not correct, when the app is installed on a device, there will be an error that states **Apple ID not authorized**. To resolve this, delete the app and import into Apple Configurator with the correct Apple ID.

Deploying applications on managed devices (Become an expert)

Deploying apps on supervised devices is a similar process as with device preparation. The main difference is that when the device checks back into Apple Configurator after the initial app is deployed, the app is once again available to be assigned to devices. This means that Apple Configurator has a very unique feature not otherwise found in any solution: it allows administrators to reuse VPP codes. The ability to disassociate a VPP code and move it to a different device has a lot of different impacts to how administrators strategize around the tool; however, it comes at a cost. Devices under supervision cannot be used on other computers with iTunes.

Getting ready

Before placing an app on a device, you also need that app to appear in Apple Configurator. Therefore, make sure to have followed along with previous tasks in the book prior to attempting this one.

As we discussed in the earlier recipes, you can prepare or supervise devices. Device supervision removes the ability for a user to plug a device into iTunes, so be prepared for that.

How to do it...

Follow the given steps to get started:

1. Open Apple Configurator.
2. Click on **Supervise** in the top row of icons.
3. From the **Supervise** screen, click on a group of supervised devices in the left sidebar.
4. Highlight a device in the center column as shown in the following screenshot:

5. Check the box for the application(s) you want to install on the devices.

6. Click on **Refresh** at the bottom of the screen, making sure devices are docked in the process.

There's more...

Managing an Apple device efficiently is just part of the task. Supervision is also a major necessity to ensure smooth functioning of the device.

Device supervision and assignment

Device supervision allows administrators to apply codes for apps to devices and then take them back, when the device gets checked, into Apple Configurator. However, assigning devices take this paradigm to a new level and allows administrators to assign documents to these apps. Stay tuned, as we cover doing so in the *Adding files to devices (Should know)* recipe.

Adding files to devices (Should know)

Whether for one or multiple users/devices, sometimes it is necessary to add files to one or many devices. Here we go through adding content to our devices as well as recommending best practices for adding different types of files.

Getting ready

In order to add different types of content to our devices, we need to have an application installed on the device that can open that type of file. You will also need to make sure that users are created in Apple Configurator.

For example, to open a PDF file we need an application that can open PDFs on the device. You can read about installing applications in the *Deploying applications on prepared devices (Become an expert)* recipe.

How to do it...

To get started, make sure that your devices are under supervision. We talk in depth about supervision and assigning devices in the *Deciding whether to prepare, supervise, or assign (Must know)* recipe.

1. To get started, click on the **Assign** button in the Configurator pane. Once in the **Assign** pane, you will see that there are three distinct areas:

   - **Groups**
   - **Users**
   - **Documents**

2. Choose the user that you will be assigning documents to by highlighting the user in the **Users** section.

3. Once the user is highlighted, click on the plus [**+**] sign in the bottom-left corner of the **Documents** section.

 You can only put files on the device if you have already installed an application that can open that type of document and it has iTunes files sharing capabilities.

You will now be prompted with a choice of the application that you want to open the file with.

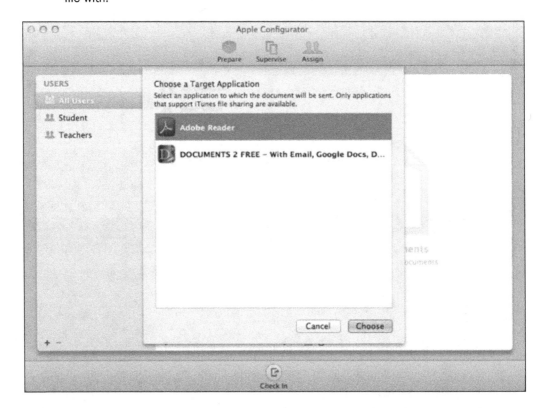

 There are several free applications out there such as Adobe Reader and Documents 2 Free. Please test these before deployment.

4. When you click on **Choose**, you will be prompted to find the file on your computer to be opened.

5. Click on **Open**.

    You can do this for several files and they will be added onto your device.

6. When all of the files are added to the window, click on **Check Out**.

Now the application used to open the document is in the file list.

How it works...

Configurator takes advantage of the same file transfer system as iTunes to move files into the applications. Only applications that have the capability to open files in this manner will work to transfer documents and files onto the device.

> You must install an application via Configurator and the application must have the iTunes file transfer capability built in. If the app does not have this feature built in, it will not show up in the list of applications.
>
> Also remember you can remove files in the same way by clicking on the minus button in the documents pane.

Importing files back to the computer (Should know)

Sometimes it will be important to receive documents from a user or a device. Some examples include forms, worksheets, or user-created content. This can easily be done with Apple Configurator.

Getting ready

In order to pull documents/files from devices, the applications that are in use must be installed via Configurator. You can learn how to install applications by reading the installing applications section. To retrieve documents, you must also check the device out to a user.

How to do it...

To get started, make sure that your devices are under supervision. We talk in depth about supervision and assigning devices in the *Deciding whether to prepare, supervise, or assign (Must know)* recipe.

1. Connect the assigned device to your computer.
2. Open Configurator.
3. Click on **Check In**.

   When the device is checked in, you will see the list of files in the documents pane.

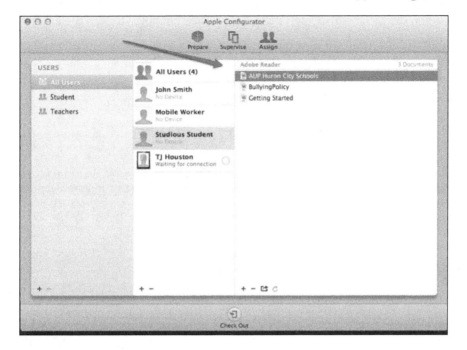

4. Click on the Export button at the bottom of the documents pane. (This button looks like the share button in iOS and Mountain Lion.)

5. When you click on the Export button, you will be prompted to save the document.

6. Give the file a name and click on Export.

7. Remember to give the document a unique name so you do not get files confused if you are doing this for multiple users.

8. You can now open the file on your computer and view the document.

How it works...

Configurator takes advantage of the same file transfer system as iTunes to move files into applications. Only applications that are capable of opening files in this manner work to transfer documents and files onto devices.

Thank you for buying
Instant Apple Configurator How-to

About Packt Publishing

Packt, pronounced 'packed', published its first book "*Mastering phpMyAdmin for Effective MySQL Management*" in April 2004 and subsequently continued to specialize in publishing highly focused books on specific technologies and solutions.

Our books and publications share the experiences of your fellow IT professionals in adapting and customizing today's systems, applications, and frameworks. Our solution based books give you the knowledge and power to customize the software and technologies you're using to get the job done. Packt books are more specific and less general than the IT books you have seen in the past. Our unique business model allows us to bring you more focused information, giving you more of what you need to know, and less of what you don't.

Packt is a modern, yet unique publishing company, which focuses on producing quality, cutting-edge books for communities of developers, administrators, and newbies alike. For more information, please visit our website: www.packtpub.com.

Writing for Packt

We welcome all inquiries from people who are interested in authoring. Book proposals should be sent to author@packtpub.com. If your book idea is still at an early stage and you would like to discuss it first before writing a formal book proposal, contact us; one of our commissioning editors will get in touch with you.

We're not just looking for published authors; if you have strong technical skills but no writing experience, our experienced editors can help you develop a writing career, or simply get some additional reward for your expertise.

PUBLISHING

Instant Apple iBooks How-to

ISBN: 978-1-849694-02-5   Paperback: 52 pages

Learn how to read and write books for iBookstore, by fully utilizing Apple iBooks and iBooks Author

1. Learn something new in an Instant! A short, fast, focused guide delivering immediate results.

2. Learn everything you need know, from reading iBooks to creating and publishing your own

3. Presented in an easy-to-follow tutorial style, this book is your quick and compact guide to iBooks

iWork for Mac OS X Cookbook

ISBN: 978-1-849693-10-3   Paperback: 324 pages

Over 50 recipes which go beyond the manuals and explore the incredible potential of iWork to do the job of a full creative suite

1. Explodes the widely held view that iWork is simply Apple's version of MS Office by revealing the amazing creative power of this office suite

2. Use iWork to create high quality documents for professional printing or internet use

3. Written for both the new and experienced iWork user, this book is a step-by-step guide to creating dazzling graphics, unique clip art, logos, and sophisticated designs to rival top-end professional programs

Please check **www.PacktPub.com** for information on our titles

Instant New iPad Features in iOS 6 How-to

ISBN: 978-1-782160-46-5   Paperback: 74 pages

Learn to use Mail, iCloud, Photo Stream, iPhoto, iWorks, iTunes, iMovie, and Garageband through easy-to-follow recipes

1. Learn something new in an Instant! A short, fast, focused guide delivering immediate results.

2. Set up Mail using multiple accounts and a VIP Inbox

3. Enable iCloud for synchronous use with other Apple devices and programs

iOS 5 Essentials

ISBN: 978-1-849692-26-7   Paperback: 252 pages

Harness iOS 5's new powerful features to create stunning applications

1. Integrate iCloud, Twitter and AirPlay into your applications.

2. Lots of step-by-step examples, images and diagrams to get you up to speed in no time with helpful hints along the way.

3. Each chapter explains iOS 5's new features in-depth, whilst providing you with enough practical examples to help incorporate these features in your apps

Please check **www.PacktPub.com** for information on our titles

www.ingramcontent.com/pod-product-compliance
Lightning Source LLC
LaVergne TN
LVHW080103070326
832902LV00014B/2391